A New Beginning

A Woman's Guide To Self Respect In Order To Make A Stand

- *Prevention Of Domestic Violence*
- *Learn To Respect Yourself*
- *Learn To Respect Others*
- *Learn To Make The Opposite Sex Respect You*
- *Learn To Gain Respect From Others*

Madena Williams

authorHOUSE®

AuthorHouse™
1663 Liberty Drive, Suite 200
Bloomington, IN 47403
www.authorhouse.com
Phone: 1-800-839-8640

First published by AuthorHouse 9/9/2008

ISBN: 978-1-4389-0742-0 (sc)

Printed in the United States of America
Bloomington, Indiana

This book is printed on acid-free paper.

For information or to order additional books, Write to:

MG Resources

2305 Park Ave. Ste. 1208

Detroit, Mi. 48201

Author's Note

For many generations, females have been trying to make a man respect them, and to receive respect from others. It is a fact, that many females still have to learn how to respect themselves, and then they can expect society to respect them. It is also a proven fact, that females have got to stop walking around with a chip on their shoulders, and start to give respect to others. Having nasty attitudes won't get you the respect you the female acquire. Being loud and obnoxious is in that same category.

Using people isn't the way to go either. Once you use a person, the favor will return back to you. I guarantee that you won't like the results. Using a man for his money doesn't have a good return policy either; you will fail in the end, and you can't blame anyone else but yourself.

Everything you the reader find in this publication, may help in every part of your life. There are going to be women who will say, there isn't anything wrong with their life. Most women who say that, didn't even make a thorough check of their life. Usually if a female takes the time to check herself, she will find some adjustments can be made. Will she make the adjustments? She may or she may not correct herself. One thing for sure, the information is here for all females to take advantage of. It is private, it is serious, and on some occasions it is down right mean. This publication wasn't written to make fun of anyone at all. It was written for the females to think about what they are doing, to have better success in their relationship, and to make personal changes. Over all, this publication can assist in improving one's life for the better.

I hope you the reader enjoy the reading, find some answers for yourself, and find a better you.

Contents

Females Have Forgotten How To Be A Lady 1

For Women in All Cultures It's Time To Make A Change......................8

It Doesn't Hurt To Smile It Doesn't Hurt To Say Hello.......................11

Talking About Him Isn't The Same As Doing His Will.........................14

Food For Thought 17

What Has Happened To Our Elders?...20

Women In All Cultures It's Time To Stop Letting Men Make You Look Like Idiots! 25

Stop Letting Your Man Have His Cake And Eat It Too!......................29

Colors 35

Review Of The Difficult Females..37

What Makes Females Attracted To Bad Boys?...................................40

Recap On What Females Have To Remember....................................42

SIGNS..47

Long Winded Females Shut Up!...51

When A Man Takes You For Granted The Signs Will Be There............54

Understanding The Basics...61

Things To Keep Out Of Your Relationship Verbal and Physical Abuse 63

Females Have Forgotten How To Be A Lady

The current year is 2007, and some of the females have forgotten how to be ladies. Some of the females dress like sluts, and if someone says something about it, then they have the nerve to have an attitude. Here are some suggestions (I know that you *aren't going to do it, but I am going to tell you anyway*). You are really pathetic showing all of your skin just to catch a man. The only thing it proves is that you have no social skills at all. When a female has to shows what she has to catch a man, and he falls for it, what makes you think he won't be attracted to someone else the same way? The only thing that a man wants to do is to have sex, then move on to the next female; then you say (with your actions) it's ok. Did you ever think about how many other women he has slept with? I have one thing to tell you sister, a real man doesn't want a tainted female. I'm going to tell you that right now. So you better start cleaning your stuff up.

Nails can look very nice if they are the right length. I have seen some nails that look nasty (*underneath*), and the nails are too long period. For the women who have nails that long, I would like to know how do you clean yourself? I know some females don't

clean themselves very good, but you have got to admit that your stuff isn't all that clean if your nails are that long. I have seen nails so long till all 10 curves, and the female has to grab things with her knuckles. This is just a pitiful sight to see. Being ghetto is too common now. For the woman who wants to do better for herself, you can listen to what I have to say. You see more ghetto females than enough on your journey through life.

The only thing that you can do at this point is to stay away from them. Most of them are loud, obnoxious, can cuss like a sailor (*figure of speech*), and they want to know why they can't have a decent relationship.

Everything that I have mentioned so far, are some of the reasons why males do not respect a woman. You see, when you show a man that you are a respectable woman, then he will treat you like one; if not then you have the wrong male companion.

The one thing that women have the tendency of doing, is letting men do them wrong. When all hell breaks loose, they want to put the blame on the men instead of themselves. Here is an example:

A woman owns her own house, and she has her boyfriend live with her. She can't get any money from him at all to help pay the rent /mortgage; but she continues to let him stay in her home. She herself hasn't paid the rent/ mortgage either. Now she has lost the house, and she blames him for her down fall. This is one of the stupidest things a woman can do to herself. The following message is for the women who blame their mates for their down fall.

A SPECIAL MESSAGE PLEASE PAY ATTENTION

Whether you are a ghetto female or not, you have some things to change in your life <u>ASAP</u>. When you have something that belongs to you and only you, there are special duties that you must perform, and no one but you should perform those duties. If you have property in your name, you are responsible for that piece of property not your boyfriend. If you let your boyfriend move in and he isn't helping you with your rent / mortgage, then he has got to go live somewhere else. If you let him stay in your home, and you can't make the payments, then it isn't his fault it is yours. You ask "Why is it your fault?", because you were the one who let him stay in your home without him helping with the bills. You were the one who let him stay there in your home. You fussed and argued with him about not helping out with the bills; yet you still let him stay in your home smoking, drinking, and just freeloading off of you. I must say to you that you need to stop yelling at him, and start yelling at yourself. You should have common sense enough to know that you control the situation not him. You knew from the beginning that he wasn't giving up anything to you, and you knew he didn't treat you right in the first place. So bottom line, you got what you deserved. Why do I say that? Because you knew all along that he wasn't any good to you in the first place. He played you like a puppet on a string, and you let him. Take it from me, I love sex like the next person; but sex doesn't pay the bills, and you should know that by now. If you are going to cuss someone out, then go to the mirror and let loose. Get my point?

Whether a man is ghetto or not, a man can only do what you let him do. I don't care what culture or what beliefs a person has in our

3

country, this belief <u>should be</u> universal. When a female presents herself as a bitch, then you will be treated like a bitch. If a female presents herself like a slut, then she will be treated like a slut. If you like to drink alcohol and you change for the worse, then you should expect to be treated very badly. If you the female have a sour mouth, like cussing (*every other word is a cuss word*), being loud, thinking that you'll tell anyone off, out spoken in a negative way, then you're not to be respected at all. The female who believes she is all that, well you're not. For every female who acts ghetto (*there is ghetto in all cultures*), you need to stop your actions. Actions such as cussing (*you can get your point across without it*), getting loud (*you make yourself look stupid*), checking other people when you need to check yourself (*just because your life is screwed up, that doesn't mean that you can spread your poison to everyone else*). Wait! I am not finished.

For the PLUS SIZE WOMEN! (*I am pointing my finger at the women who are insensitive. Please remember that.*) There are certain plus sized women who want to spread their poison to other people. When I say poison, I mean these females talk about people in a bad way. These women talk about what other people look like, they talk about other people's lives, and call them names for no reason what so ever. I am aiming right at you, the female who has talked about people for no reason at all. I think that you need to stop and think about your own situation. You see, there are some who can't hold on to their own relationship, and so they want to try to ruin someone else's relationship. Yes, there are a lot of women out there in the world who want to see other females fail in their relationship.

First off, you the PLUS SIZE woman who is trying to make other people miserable (*we all know who you are*), what makes you think that you are better than anybody else? You can't talk about anyone. Picture this scene, you are in a restaurant talking about someone like a dog, and you are loud with your comments. This is how someone else sees you: There is a big fat sow with two, three, even four rolls of fat bulging from her sides, her stomach is so big, her stomach stops her from sitting close to the table in front of her so she eat. Not only that, her tits has become crumb catchers. The chair you are sitting in isn't big enough for you because your fat hangs over it. But yet you have the nerve to talk about other people, and get loud with it. That is ghetto!

(Please understand that there are people with medical problems, and they have no choice but to be a PLUS SIZE. Also there are really nice plus sized women who are very nice, and a joy to be around.) (They have nice hygiene, and they know how to treat other people. These women maybe going through hell, but they keep it to themselves, and they aren't ghetto.) My point to you is, stop tormenting other people with your negativity, and take the time to clean your life up. If you were cleaning up your own life, you wouldn't have time to create havoc in someone else's life. Yes, the same goes for skinny females also. Yes, they have a mouth on them too. Remember, if all of you want to be treated like a descent woman, then do the right thing and act like one.

The one thing all females should have had is home training. If you weren't lucky enough to have someone in your life to teach you how to become a non-mouthy, non-cussing, or even non-stinky person *(like your underarms, your vagina, and your butt)*, then you need to start learning how to do these things. *(Gentleman still do exist, and the reason why you don't know that, is because you are not a descent woman). (Are you pissed about what I just said? Don't be pissed at what I've said, because you the female who doesn't keep her hygiene up need a reality check).* You see, if a man likes to smell a female who is funky, then that is a nasty idiot. This type of man don't care about who he kisses, or what he sucks on. You know what I am talking about. This is what you call a disgusting female and a disgusting male. So now you the female can't say that no one told you the real story. As I said before clean up your act. Stop wearing clothes that are too tight. It looks like you are trying to get back into your school age clothes. Baby, those days are over with. Just because you squeezed into a smaller size, that doesn't mean you loss weight. Those threads are popping like hell. Also, it is bad when you have to wear men jeans because you are too big *(if you have a medical condition then it is understandable).* So cut the attitude.

Speaking about clothes too tight or too short, what is with these females going to casinos, wearing summertime clothes, with winter coats? These young adult females need to get a grip. They want to attract men so bad, they will do anything to get their attention. Just remember, while you are flaunting your little stuff, somebody has the same as you, but bigger and better. A female who does this type of advertising, life is going to kick you ass *(sorry for the language).*

For the females who were taught by their mothers in a wise way, do what they say. You will be surprised at how many men actually like descent females. Remember, a man can only do what you let him do. Take control of yourself, and be strong. If the male is forcing the word yes and you are saying no, then you have to enforce the word no. Stick to what you are saying to him. If he gets violent, then you have to take the next step and get the law enforcement involved (*for those of you who don't know what I am saying, you have to call the police*).

Another thing that all females have to understand is, if you respect yourself and other people, you will be respected by others. You see ghetto women everyday in different cultures, and it isn't a pretty sight. All females should show some class about themselves, and when you do you'll be surprised how much respect you will receive from society.

For Women in All Cultures
It's Time To Make A Change

I know that there are many women who believe in being clean, respectable, and they know how to treat other people with respect. But there are certain women who don't know how to be clean or be respectable. Please pay attention to what I am about to say. Many women will be able to relate to the different types of situations I will speak about, because they either do it themselves, or they have seen it done.

Many times females use paper towel to open the bathroom door in many establishments. Do you want to know why? Respectable women are using paper towel to open the bathroom door when exiting. There are many women who go to the bathroom, and don't wash their hands. These women sit on the toilet (*it doesn't matter if you stand either*) they urinate, they have bowel movements, and they have to wipe their vagina and butt off. When females do this, they have stinky fingers that smells like either fish, ammonia or butt crack. When you wipe your butt off from stool, you may have some brown stuff on your hands somewhere. Because of these mishaps, all females should wash their hands. There are so many females who don't wash their hands, and they have the nerve to touch other people. (*I myself have experienced females using the bathroom, not washing their hands before leaving, and they touched other people in their faces, or kiss little children. I strongly believe that is very trifling. Furthermore, that is why you don't eat everyone's cooking, and if people have a cooking business out of there home, it is illegal. You can't have a business like that operating from your home, because of sanitation reasons. Just an FYI for everyone.)*

To the women who do wash there hands, I just want to say thank you for remembering what mama taught you; and for the women who just put water on their hands, my question to you is what makes you think your hands are clean? The only thing you are doing is spreading your germs around on your hands. Please for your sake and everyone else's, wash your hands with soap and water. If your hands get dry when you wash them, then use lotion. Do you get my meaning? I hope you do and I hope you change.

Females who tinkle on the toilet seat in the different establishments, will you please clean up your urine? It came from you, it's yours, so what is the problem? Let me teach you the correct way to clean it off. All you have to do is take a piece of toilet paper and wipe it off. The same thing is done when you are on your period. The one thing that can help you not to tinkle on the toilet seat, is to trim your hairs around the vagina area, and around the lip part. You see, when a female urinates, the strands of hair causes the urine to drip different ways. So when you get up from the toilet you are still dripping and it hits the seat. It is normal for that to happen. You know as well as I do, that there is a lot to being a female. We all have to take care of our bodies, and we have to show pride in our lives. I don't care if other females do the same nasty habits. Everyone will not do the right thing as far as hygiene is concerned. There will be trifling people in the world, but you don't have to be one of them. I hope that I shed some light on the issues that some women have trouble with. I don't mean to down anyone at all. I figure that if I help females understand what they don't pay attention to, then maybe they will start to pay more attention to what they do. After all, our mothers taught us better than to disrespect ourselves and others. Many mothers have passed on, and their teachings should live forever. Ladies, bring respect back to us all. If every woman stands up for herself, society will have a new outlook on the female race. Not every female will have self respect, but we can start with ourselves.

It Doesn't Hurt To Smile
It Doesn't Hurt To Say Hello

How many times have you passed a female in public, she looks at you like you did something to her? There are some females who are as nice as can be. In passing, they say hello to other females, or just a smile as if to say hello. I like that type of atmosphere myself. *(I have said hello to black females, and they look at me as if to say "Why you say something to me?" Not all black females have nasty attitudes, but the ones that do need an attitude adjustment. For the Black females who need an attitude adjustment, you need to stop thinking that just because you can act like a bitch, people should be afraid of you. Also, just because you can get loud and tell someone off, that doesn't mean anything. Remember that if you raise hell, act like a bitch in public, there are other women who can do it better than you. Also, most of the Black females have the nerve to get upset when the Black man goes to another race. Well, ask yourselves something. Why should the Black man stay in the race when I am acting like a bitch? You see, it isn't about who got the best shape, the best tits, or the best looking ass, it is about how do you carry yourself? If you want the Black man to come back to the race, then give him a reason to come back. If the Black females don't give the Black man reasons to stay in the race, then the females do not have the right to say anything. Just because the Black man likes to see the Black women half naked, that doesn't mean you give them what they want. It is ok to look nice and sexy, but there is a limit. Remember, you can train any man to respect you. If you say that you can't, then that means you rather be treated badly. If you want a good man, then you have to work at it like everything else in life, and that is just the way it is. If you want to be respected by society, then you need to stop bitching and start changing. When you begin to change, the Black female race can rise as a whole and be respected by all. If you are a Black female and you're not ghetto, then you have won half the battle.)*

Relationships

It's Time For A Change!

For Adults Only

- Read what some are afraid to talk about.
- You may look at others in a different light.
- Nasty habits that could be in your back yard.
- Are you happy?
- Do you deserve better?
- Would you believe that life is what you make it?
- Do people treat you nicely?
- Do you ever have a pleasant look on your face?
- Do you whine all the time?
- Do you respect yourself?
- Do you respect others?

If you are not happy with your life, then what are
you going to do about it?
Think About It!

See ordering information inside this publication

Talking About Him Isn't The Same As Doing His Will

There are many people who believe that if you talk about God then that is enough. Many of the females know of God, but they don't practice His will. Ladies, please pay attention to the inspiration that I will bring to you. You just might understand what I am saying.

The one thing that society does that makes me sick, is the forcing of religion on a person. They feel they will get highly noticed if they are bringing in a lot of new comers to the church. You will find some congregations actually forcing there beliefs on an individual, and that is not the way to go about it. The way society is this day and time, it is a race to get the congregation to be as big as possible. NOT ALL OF SOCIETY PUSHES RELIGION ON A PERSON, BUT THERE IS ENOUGH OF SOCIETY THAT DOES.

You see, I believe that everyone has forgotten that the belief in God has to be FREE WILL. If a person is forced to believe in God, then that wouldn't be any good to God. The words fake belief comes into mind, and God may not accept the beliefs of the individual who is being pushed. If you are going to preach to people about God, then you have to be prepared yourself. How do you prepare yourself for such a serious subject? Well, you have to make sure that you are following God's will the best way you can. Live His words the best way you can. What ever you don't understand about God, please do not make up things. Do the research, and then come to your own conclusions. The one thing that I know that God is against, is arguing over religion.

You see, arguing over someone's beliefs is really stupid! If that person believes in something totally different from what you believe in, then leave it alone! The same goes for the other person as well. God doesn't tolerate arguing over religion. My question is, why even bother raising your blood pressure over something you can't control? Always remember that you can't control other people's beliefs, and that is just the way it is.

Let's talk a little bit more about free will so you the reader can get an even better idea of what I am talking about. You are an adult, and you have the freedom to do as you please (as long as it is legal). Example: *(You have a friend who keeps bothering you about signing up at a fitness company. You have already made up in your mind that you don't want to join. Your friend keeps hounding you and hounding you. Then one day you decided to sign up for the fitness club, knowing that you have to pay whether you go or not. The only reason why you signed up for the membership, so your friend can shut up about the fitness club.)*

Do you see what just happened to this situation? If you didn't then go back and reread it so you can get a full understanding. You see, you didn't want to sign up for a fitness club in the first place. But your friend kept hounding you for quite awhile, so you signed up just to shut your friend's mouth up. This situation wasn't free will at all. The mere fact that your friend kept pushing makes it not free will at all. Now you are stuck with an unwanted bill, all because your friend kept pushing you to sign up. Free will would have been if you signed up without pressure from your friend.

God tolerates only free will. All of us have to come to Him willingly and not pushed to Him. You go to Him when everything is going well, and you go to Him when everything is over whelming. It really isn't hard to do. Just privately be to yourself, and just talk to Him. You can't see Him, but you can feel Him. After all, believing in Him has to be free will.

Food For Thought

It is understood that when a person turns to God in times of need, it has to be free will. I must make it clear to people that you don't just go to God when you're in trouble. I hate to say this, but you may be ignored. The reason for this is because God isn't a toy that you can take out of a box and say "Ok God do your thing, and get me out of this mess." Then when He is done, you put Him back in His box. It doesn't work that way people! For the ones who think it does, you have the never to get mad when He doesn't do anything. My question to you is, what did you actually think was going to happen? You have to be with God 24/7 and that is the bottom line.

Let me tell you how it works. (*You can believe this or not, it really is up to you.*) When a person has decided to praise God and accept Jesus as their savior, you then must spiritually keep in contact with them both all the time. (*Some people believe in God and Jesus being separate, or the both are as one; it depends on your beliefs. REMEMBER WE ARE HERE TO LEARN NOT ARGUE. Keep your beliefs to yourself and just listen.*) You can start by saying thank you Lord for letting me wake up this morning, thank Him for the meals you have received, thank the Lord for being in your life. Pray to him every morning to bless you all day, and to have blessings come to you all the time. Tell Him you love Him and mean it! Small things like that would make Him happy. In other words, get closer to Him or shell I say them.

Try to remember that you have to be with God from the beginning, and not just when you get into trouble. If you do then you may sink. Please don't be like some people where they praise God, and they're still acting hellish. NOT GOOD!

For those who want to blame their problems on other people, I must tell you that you are really the cause of your own down fall. Fix your own problems they don't belong to anyone else but you.
The rest of us have enough of our own problems.
You are responsible for your own problems, so please act like it!

Problems that have to be fixed

Just think if all of your problems were in this box, you could alleviate them in a heart-beat.
That would be the perfect idea wouldn't it?

What Has Happened To Our Elders?

It doesn't matter what culture you are in, the elders need to be talked to also. I must admit that I am a Baby Boomer, and as I remember the elders *(lets say 50 and up)* had so much knowledge to give. You can listen to them and it seemed like they had all the answers. The only reason why it seemed that way was because they were much older, and they have already been where others are going. So the elders were believed to be much wiser than all of us. The elders had the answers to life, and by them spreading knowledge that they already obtained, it would help the next generations to come. Don't get me wrong life was still hard, and people still had to struggle to make a living. The time period that is being talked about ranges from 1946 to 1964 (Baby Boomer period). Let's go beyond 1964. The elders were gaining more and more knowledge. The different generations that were existing, had only two choices. Those choices were either listen and do what your parents say or get out. Most parents/grandparents were very strict with their teachings, and if you didn't follow it, then you got a butt whipping.

Grandparents taught their children and grandchildren how to become respectable men and women. In other words, parents took charge of their children, and grandparents made sure their teachings were being enforced. It is true that you had some grandparents who needed to be retrained on life, but it wasn't that many. It is also true that some parents didn't give a damn what their children did, just as long as they were out of the house *(and they have the nerve to say their children weren't bad)*. Yes, it is true that some grandparents did the same thing, but the majority of the parents/grandparents took responsibility, and raised those children responsibly. Yes, it is easy to gap your legs open, but it isn't easy raising children.

Some may say that not all of the older people had common sense back then. I believe that statement applies in every generation. Everyone should know that there are desirable and undesirable people in all cultures. So if a person comes across another who doesn't have that much knowledge, then it is up to that individual if they should follow the other person's advice or not. It is true that some elders are not able to give advice on anything. Fortunately, there are a lot of elders who can still lead us.

Another thing that I would like to touch base on is, there are elders who still do bad habits in home and out in public. They too don't wash their hands like they're suppose to, they put there hands in food, lick their fingers, and put it back in the food that is meant for the public. It is just pitiful how some people just don't use common sense. When I say common sense I mean, think about what you were taught. Let's take food for example: *(this really does happen)* there is an elder at a buffet, and she /he decides to use their fork instead of the large ladle, or spoon that was intended for self serve. If they do use the prongs or ladles that were meant for the specific foods, they may put the ladle or prong in their mouths. Here is where common sense should be used. Before putting something like that in your mouth, just ask yourself this question. Would you want someone else putting their mouth on something that you will be choosing to purchase? Would you like it if someone else put their fingers in the food that you were going to eat? How about seeing someone putting their fingers in their mouth, and then putting their fingers back in the food? I will tell you how you would feel, you would be mad as hell, you would talk about that person, and you may even report that person to management. So you the elder, who does this sort of thing, think about how you would feel if someone did that to you. After all, you are too old to be doing something that rude. Your parents taught you better than that. You are an elder whether you like it or not. You the elder who needs to be retrained about having manners, and respect for others need to start right away.

While I am talking about retraining for certain elders, you need to learn that just because you are an elder, that doesn't give you the right to cuss people out on a whim, or disrespect other people in society. Yes, it is true that you have been through hell in life, but it should be your mission to set a good example for others to follow. These are the same rules we all grew up with. If you the elder didn't grow up with these rules, I truly feel for you. But that is no excuse at all. You should know that life is a great teacher, and the object is to listen, learn and then apply.

You have read about how elders can be considered 50 and up. Now let's look at 30s and 40s, and how people in this age range can be considered elders. Let me explain what I mean. You see, people in their 20s have to have some type of role models, and people in their 30s have role models, and the same with the rest of the age groups. Ask yourself how can a person mature by themselves? The answer is, by seeing others operating in society. How would you know that you have to be well groomed for an interview, if you didn't see others well groomed at an interview? What about respect for others? You respect others because you were taught to respect others (*hopefully*), and you see others respecting each other. So my point is, every generation has elders. Some of the elders are good and some are bad. Pay attention to the good ones, and you will see that you will make it through life. Always remember that life isn't always what you make it. Life can have a lot of rocky roads, and you have to decide which one you will take in order for you to succeed in life.

Words Of Wisdom Can Go Along Way

No matter what ladies, the information in this publication is for someone who is in search of changing their lives around. From young to elder, you can either change your life around, or you can spread the news that there is a way to change. It is true that it is hard to see the light when you are in a bad situation yourself. It takes someone else to see what you can't see, and then they can show you the correct way to go.

*As always, be careful who you trustwith your personal business. Not everyone should be trusted.

Women In All Cultures
It's Time To Stop Letting Men
Make You Look Like Idiots!

We need to talk ladies. For many years, men were aloud to get away with playing around on a woman. Then he justifies the action, you take him back, then you go after the female he is playing around with. It is time to change the cycle. Women fight over their men, destroy property over their men, even kill over their men, and for what purpose? He wasn't that great in the first place. If he was, then he wouldn't have placed you in that position in the first place. Did you get what I just said? "HE WOULDN'T HAVE PLACED YOU IN THAT POSITION IN THE FIRST PLACE IF HE WAS SO GREAT!" You need to play that phrase over and over again in your mind until you get the picture. After all, if your man is playing around on you, you need to take a good long look at the situation and make a decision (*staying with him isn't the answer*).

He cries, he says he is sorry, he says he won't do it again. You feel sorry for him, and the next thing you know some months later, he is playing around on you again. Only this time a baby was made with the other relationship. So what are you going to do, go after the other woman? If your answer is yes, then my question to you is why? Did the other woman stalk the both of you? Did the other woman put a gun to his head and say "Be with me"? Is this the first time you've seen this woman before? Take a good look at this situation. I say leave the other woman alone. Your man was the one who stepped out on you, he is the one who betrayed your trust, and he is the one who wanted to be taken. What I have just said makes a lot of sense. Remember that a man can't be taken from a relationship unless he wants to be taken. When your man does this to you, you look like an idiot fighting over your man who doesn't want you any more.

I guess it is a woman's nature that women act the way they do. Love can make you do some stupid shit (*all of us need to use our heads*). This is why you have to rule with your mind. You the female, have got to stop convincing yourself that you love your man so much, till you let him run over you. Remember these words: BEING IN LOVE DOESN'T HAVE TO MEAN BEING STUPID. These are words to live by. It is important that you listen to them when you recite them to yourself. If your man is playing around it is time to leave him! He isn't going to stop with one, and you know that! So why keep putting yourself in heavy misery? He will say he won't do it again, and he'll say no baby this, no baby that! It is time to leave him bottom line. Just like if he put his hand on you, it is most defiantly time to go (*don't make him put his hand on you either, you know what I am talking about*).

Ladies who are in their 20s, you are still two young to understand, but you really need this advice also. You see, you still have childish ways, and you still can't think straight. You still want to fight over your man or (*he really isn't your man if you have to fight over him*) shall I say boy? He has been making you look like a fool for a long time, and now it is coming out. Have you ever heard your parents say "What is done in the dark, comes out in the light?" That phrase is true. Who ever started that phrase, said a mouthful.

It is true that girls in elementary school start to look at boys, and then if another little girl likes the same boy, then there is a problem. Then you have Junior High School girls *(teens)*, they go for blood. Then High School age *(they go for blood too)*. None of the girls stop to think that they are making themselves look like fools. If they had any sense, they would make the boys look like idiots; that would be a good change.

Unfortunately, these boys grow up to be men, and they keep the same childish ways. Women going after each other, while the men are making moves on other females, and these females aren't aware of his past or the present. This is what the females have got to stop doing. They have got to stop letting men make them look like idiots. It has been a problem for a long time, and females have the ability to put these men in their place once and for all. Please remember that a man can only do what you let him do.

By all means stop playing games. When you play games with a male, you could be setting yourself up for a fall. Males can be dirty, and will get you back in a way you can't recover. It is true that there are no easy answers, but you can start to practice on having a better life without the drama.

To all females no matter the age, you have to stop complaining, and start making a stand for yourselves. You don't have to cuss, you don't have to show out, and you don't have to badger him *(you don't look like the victim any more)*. Not all females will follow these suggestions, but the ones that will, you have a chance to become a better person. Do not let the male race take your dignity away. If you live in the U.S.A., then you have a chance to override him in every way.

If you live with your man who is acting up, then you have got to make plans to save some money and get out of the relationship. You may be in a position where you can't leave, because you have no where to go. If this is the position that you are in, then you may have to go to a shelter *(even if you have kids)*. You may not like that move, but at least it is a move. Sometimes you have to make sudden decisions, in order to stop the violence that is going on. There is no reason to stay. By the love of God, don't say "But I love him." You have got to break out of that mode, and save yourself before you won't be able to. If there are kids involved, then you have all the more reason to leave the situation at hand. It isn't easy, but you will win if you think things through.

Stop Letting Your Man Have His Cake And Eat It Too!

Let's continue the lesson shell we? One thing that some men like to do is to do wrong purposely, and then pacify you so you won't bitch so bad. I want the reader to pay attention to the next important information I have to say. Hopefully you are strong enough to do it.

For those of you who have men who like to step out on the relationship, I have to ask you why do you let it happen? You may say "There isn't anything I can do about that at all." Yes, there is something that you can do about that situation. Totally leave him. If you stay with him, then you telling him that it is ok for him to see other people, while being with you. You are also telling him that it is ok to run over you, and I'm going to love you no matter what. When this happens that means you don't have a relationship any more. You are just friends, and when he does something that is just unforgivable, you have no right to say anything what so ever. You the reader set the ground rules (*if this is you*), and he ran with it. You are not happy because of the situation, and I hope that you are getting money from him. I say this because that is the extent of your relationship. You are now, along with his other little friends, a prostitute with extra helpings. Don't just go by what I am saying, look at your situation. No one is to blame for what has happened to your relationship but you. The only thing I can tell you at this time is to start over, have rules for yourself, and use common sense. I will tell you how to prepare and what to watch out for. It may help you in your mission to find a decent person. There are decent men out in the world, but you have to keep your eyes open, and pay attention to your goal. It isn't going to be easy, just take your time and become friends first. You have to keep in mind that there is someone better for me out there, and I will find him. *(I don't mean a married man either. Why play second fiddle when you don't have to. If you didn't know that he was married, then that is understandable. When you find out, leave the situation because it gets worse. Look out for signs like if he has strange habits, or he just gave you his cell number, or he gave you his friend's number, or it is hard to keep up with him, or he don't call you much at all, or he makes dates and break them most of the time, and the big one is he never spends the night. He goes home at a certain time every day. If your man is doing this, then you need to really WAKE UP AND STOP BEING A DUMB ASS!)* This type of male companion is using you to the fullest. There are too many men out there in the world to choose from, to be putting up with such foolishness. You can't be that lonely, and if you are, then you need to make some new friends. How? After work, change into some nice looking not too revealing outfits *(you don't want to give the wrong signals, and remember you want a decent person)*. Please remember that a man who has money and a nice job can be an asshole too. Always be respectable. If you are not respectable, then you need to change and become respectable. You'll feel better about yourself, and people will treat you differently. *If not then the hell with them. Stop hanging around ghetto, people that is no good at all. Go to a nice social gathering, gaming places like bowling, or the mall. Be careful of bars, casinos can be ok, but you still have to be cautious. These are just some of the places that you can go to make friends. Remember friends first lovers later. Just because he is nice the first time you meet, that doesn't mean he is the one. It only means that he is a possible candidate to be friends. Don't ever rush into a relationship; you may not like the results. Look for pattern change. If the guy you meet changes, alarms should sound off in your head. Do not ignore the alarm that is going off in your head, it may be the only warning you'll receive.

Once you get a real relationship, keep everyone out of it. Stop telling everyone about the different things that happens in your relationship. When you have a fallen out, keep it between you and him. When you have sex, keep it between you and him. When you are going on a romantic trip, keep it between you and him. There are too many females who don't know how to keep their mouths shut about their own business. This is what I mean by keeping other people out of your relationship. If you are in trouble with the relationship, then that would be a different matter all together. When I say trouble I mean physical abuse, verbal abuse, mental abuse, or he is beating the children. If it is a normal relationship, then just keep things between you and him so you can work it out better. Family and friends got no business knowing what goes on between you and him sexually either *(keep your mouth shut)*.

Two situations to talk about are relationships and sports. I don't understand why some women trip out because their man is looking at sports! I say this, at least he isn't out with another, you know where he is, and you need to get a grip. Leave the man alone. At least you have him right? Let your man have his space. If you are smart, you would join him if he let you. The truth about the whole issue is, you know sport programs are coming on television, or he may go to the games. Again leave the man alone. He is with you, you guys do things together, and he can see his game in peace. You do your thing, so why can't he do his thing? While he is looking at the game go shopping, talk to friends, do some gardening, read a book, do something other than bother him when he is looking at sports. You also can join him in looking at the game. Let him have a buddy at home he can talk to about the game *(I mean you being his buddy)*.

INGREDIENTS FOR A GOOD RELATIONSHIP

- Good Communication Between The Both Of You
- Respect For Each Other Beliefs
- Respecting Each Other In Public and Privately
- Trusting Each Other (Don't Abuse Each Others Trust)
- Understanding Each Others Character
- Motivation To Be Happy With Each Other
  (When you treat each other correctly, that is motivation to be happy.)
- Love (Love is never first)

If you have the ingredients listed above in your relationship, then you have a good base for a good and strong relationship. The secret could be that both partners have to maintain these good qualities through the entire relationship. Yes, in some cases it is easier said than done, but with both partners working towards a good relationship it will work.

Still have doubts?
Ask yourself "Is my partner worth the effort?"
If not then you know what to do.

Write down your thoughts about your
relationship both bad and good below.
Then weigh your options.
(Trying to get you to see what could be wrong.)

Colors

Have you ever thought about how colors affect you? Colors can be vibrant, colors can be dull. The one thing I want you to explore is, how does color make you feel inside? Do you feel a difference when you put your clothes on, do you feel a difference when you touch a certain color, or are you so busy that you haven't noticed?

Believe it or not, color could be responsible for the way you feel in the morning, afternoon, and at night. You have your bright colors like red, royal blue, yellow, green, and orange. Let's work with these colors. If you mix these colors together, you will have a beautiful array of colors that are bright and happy. Now I want you to figure out what these colors do for you? When you can go to the store, and pick something that has your favorite colors in it. Pay attention to how it makes you feel. Do this experiment with as many colors as you can think of. Again pay attention to how it makes you feel.

Colors are very important to how a person may feel. If you have on your favorite color, it may make you feel sexy, happy, strong, calm and serene. If you find the color that makes you feel that way, then you should invest in those items with those colors. With all the health issues with blood pressure, anxiety, and so on, you need something to help keep your nerves calm cool and collected. Also your favorite colors can help you stop mild depression. When you are down and out, try to perk yourself back up by wearing your favorite colors, or do a project with your favorite color in it. You may be surprised at the results.

Review Of The Difficult Females

So far I have talked about females and their nasty habits, their attitudes, and their self awareness practices. I have been very blunt and to the point on certain issues. If I just talk casual talk, then I wouldn't be able to get my point across to the females who need a reality check. For every female who reads this book, I hope someone has the ability to change for the better. After all, most females complain about different people disrespecting them, so I gave a solution to what could be the problem. There are so many females who want respect, but don't know how to respect themselves, in order to gain respect from others. *(Please remember, if you want respect you have to earn it!)*

Some females may get mad at what I have written in this publication, but I don't care about that. The affect of this whole publication is to speak about important issues, which others don't want to talk about. Sorry to say this, but some females love to do wrong, and don't want anyone to say anything about what they've done. Those are the females I am after. The type of females who I have mentioned in this publication, are the ones who need to be talked to. Yes, there are females who need guidance and I have supplied that road to them also.

If females want to be respected as a whole, then you have got to respect yourselves first. No female has the right to ask for respect from others, if you show that you don't respect yourself; that is just the way it is. Another issue I want to touch base on is, just because a female wears a dress that doesn't mean that she is a lady. A lot of females have this type of thinking, and I don't know who told them they would be ladies if they did, but becoming a respectable lady *(woman)* is a character, not because you wearing a dress or a sexy outfit *(a lot of females don't have the character at all).* **Please learn the difference.** Some will learn and some won't. For the female who is looking for guidance, this publication will do wonders for you. One may say "There isn't anything wrong with me." Stop setting yourself up! There is something wrong with your personality if no one is respecting you including your mate. Like I have said before, there is always something that can be changed in a person to make their life better. IF YOU STILL FEEL THAT YOU DON'T NEED TO CHANGE YOUR ATTITUDE ABOUT YOURSELF OR OTHERS, THEN PLEASE PASS THIS BOOK TO SOMEONE WHO REALLY CAN BENFIT FROM IT. There are females who really need the words that are published in this book.

For the women who are respectable, thank you for being you. Maybe other women will mimic the character. I don't think so, but I could be wrong.

So you say "There isn't any good men out in the world", or "The men don't know how to treat a lady." *(If you say one of these statements, then I have to ask how do you know there aren't any good men out in the world, when you aren't acting correctly yourself? Also, you have to be a lady to be treated like a lady. You need to remember that verse.)* Don't take my word for it, change your character/attitude and find out. You may say "I'm not changing for no one." If that is the case, then shut up complaining about the way men treat you. <u>You act like scum, trash, slut, whore, or bitch, then they are going to treat you like scum, trash, slut, whore or</u>

<u>bitch.</u> If you act like a nice decent person, a lady with a nice character, then you will be treated like that. Hang out with drug infested idiots, then you get what you get. That's the way it is. You or no other woman can change the out come period! So stop becoming part of the problem and start becoming part of the solution. Make your choice! FYI ladies, if other women keep thinking like what I have stated above, then we as a whole will never be able to make a stand.

What Makes Females Attracted To Bad Boys?

I believe this question goes back to maybe the 1800s and before. It could be part of the domestic violence that is happening today. Bad boys can be thugs, dope dealers *(sellers)*, gang members, ordinary men who don't take any crap from anyone. Bad boys can also be in suits. Their power may be the same as the one above, but they also have money and businesses that can make them even more powerful. I can understand how females can go for the bad boys in suits, but the scum bags and losers of the world? Ok so you have an attraction for the bad boys of your neighborhood. You get with them or you have seen other women *(who act like adolescent girls)* get with these bad boys, and their lives go to hell. Why? Because they choose to be popular in a bad way. This could also be the makings of a dysfunctional family and domestic abuse. For give my language ladies but if you have a bad boy and he kicks someone's ass, what makes you think he won't kick you ass? Didn't think about that did you? If this happens, you know damn well you won't be able to leave, unless he damn near kills you. Like I said before, for give my language. You can't run home to mom *(unless she lives in another state)*, she may be mad at you, or she may be dead. Stop running after these bad boys in the first place. You know what will happen. If you keep running after these so called bad boys, then stop complaining about the way they treat you. Stop getting use to being a punching bag. Get some help before it is too late. I believe we can't stop the violence, but we can tone it down some how. Everyone has to do their part in the prevention of domestic violence. If you catch the abuse at the beginning of the relationship, then you have a chance to leave. If you stay then you are telling your abuser that it is ok to abuse you.

Recap On What Females Have To Remember

➤ Stop acting like a hellion. Your friends hang around you not because they're your friend, but because they like seeing you make a fool of yourself, and they have something to talk about behind your back; keep thinking they're your friend. You are the butt end of their jokes. Think about it!

➤ If you want to be respected by men and society in general, then start respecting yourself. This is the only way to gain respect.

➤ Elders, you need to get back to basics. Start acting like you have home training, and start to respect again. You are the leaders *(role models)* for the rest of us. If you are still living, and still active in society, then it isn't to late to change your ways and become leaders for our tomorrows. *(Furthermore, just because you are the elderly, that doesn't mean that you have the right to disrespect others. That same rule goes for you too.) (I'm talking about the elderly who are still hell raisers. Give it a rest! Just because you are old, that doesn't mean that you can cuss out people on a whim. So straighten up and act right! By you being so close to God age wise, don't you think you need to start treating people as you would want to be treated? Think about it!)*

Just because you can tell someone off, that doesn't mean anything! You are not the only one who can tell someone off.

➤ So you got a nice body, nice tits, and a nice ass. And? What does that suppose to mean? You aren't the only one. You think that will get you respect? The only thing that will get you is a date in someone's basement, back seat of a car, in someone else's bed in a strange house you haven't seen before. Sometimes it can lead to death, and you have the nerve to holler about men not respecting you. Like I said before, if you want respect, you have to start respecting yourself. If you dress like a slut, you get treated like a slut bottom line! Dress like a lady, you get the respect you are seeking. *(You will have ghetto men talk to you, but you won't get the respect you're looking for.) (Ghetto men are in all cultures remember that!)*

➤ For the young females, why do you dress nice, look nice, hair looks nice, and start cussing? You look so stupid doing that, and then you have the nerve to say that men don't know how to respect a woman. Number one, you are not a woman. Number two, give the male race something to respect. I don't care if you are playing around when you talk to a male or female. You have to show self respect all the time. Shut up whining about men don't know how to respect a lady. YOU HAVE TO BE A LADY IN ORDER FOR THEM TO RESPECT YOU! HOW CAN YOU ASK FOR RESPECT WHEN YOU DON'T RESPECT YOURSELF? BOTTOM LINE, IF YOU WANT RESPECT, YOU HAVE TO EARN IT!

➤ When going to the bathroom, wash your hands with soap and water. You wiped yourself off from urinating, or you took a crap *(I just being nice)*, and your hands stink. Washing your hands with just water isn't washing your hands at all and you know that. Wash your hands with soap and water. Then put lotion on them. Stop making excuses why you shouldn't do this procedure!

➤ For the mean PLUS SIZE WOMEN! Stop wearing clothes like you are skinny; stop talking about people in a nasty way in public. Before you talk about someone else you need to take note of yourself. If you haven't looked in the mirror lately, maybe you need to start. After all, it isn't a pretty sight. *(You need serious help with your attitude.)*

➤ All women in general, just because you get loud, that doesn't make you right in what you are saying.

➤ Trim you pubic hairs so you don't urinate on the toilet seat. If you drip on the seat, then take tissue and wipe it up. Remember, we all know who you are. Especially if we go in the stall right behind you. Also, before you leave home, wash you vagina and you butt please. For the ones who don't, you really stink like hell! That smell lingers after you have been long gone. *(Whether your pants are up or down. You are trifling!)*

➤ If you have to use a cell phone, then pull over off the road. You don't need to use the phone while driving *(unless you have that blue tooth technology).* If not, pull over and stop trying to hit me and others on the road!

➤ *Please remember that a man can only do what you let him do. (If he treats you like crap in the beginning, and you don't correct him, then he is going to continue to treat you like crap. If you keep giving him your company when he continues to treat you like crap, then you have no right to complain. You are being stupid at that point.)* Do you get my point?

➤ When you are in a relationship, keep friends and family out off it. You can solve your problems with each other better. Family should only get involved when domestic abuse is present.

➤ Have positive communication going at all times. *(This type of communication should start at the beginning of the relationship.)*

➤ Respect each others beliefs. Respect each others space.

➤ Don't let strangers in the relationship. Keep friends out of your private life.

➤ When presenting yourself to God, it must be free will. Don't let anyone tell you different. If you are ready for God, then ask Him to help you to pick the right way to go. If you don't pick a religion, that doesn't mean that you don't believe in God. If someone tells that it does, then they are lying to you.

> ➢ Remember, speaking about God and doing His will are two different things. They should go hand and hand.

I understand that there are females who will do what they want, but there will be women who will check themselves, and try to be more aware of themselves. Those are the females who I am targeting. If a woman cares about herself, then she will make the proper adjustments to her way of life. Yes, women need guidance, and the only way it is going to happen, is for them to understand that they themselves can make the change. No one can do it for them but them. For the women who will continue being hellions, they will continue teaching other women who aren't hellions, how to respect themselves in public and behind close doors. Women will be hard headed, and they will continue to be punching bags, until they decide that maybe I and others are right. Until then, domestic abuse will be alive and well. We can't stop domestic violence, but we can tame it down. We must do it together ladies, or there will be no hope.

SIGNS

- Always remember that there are signs in almost every situation.

- There are signs that present themselves at the beginning of a relationship, and there are signs that creep through a relationship.

- Relationships can mean private, friends, business, or negative people that you deal with such as co-workers.

- Being silent is a sign.

- Action is considered a sign

- How a person speak is a sign

- What comes out a person's mouth vs. the way they act is a sign.

The one thing I hear people say all the time is "There were no signs." In many cases there are signs that a person doesn't either recognize, or ignored the signs they saw. It is important for a person to pay attention to all signs that may occur. When a person pays attention to the signs one may give, it will make them aware that something could be wrong. Once a person sees a sign of any kind, always remember that sign. More signs may be coming in the near future and you should prepare yourself.

Always remember that a relationship doesn't just mean man and woman. It can also mean friends you associate with, other people you do business with, and working with co-workers. Each of the situations above, have different results because of the nature of the relationship.

Relationship between men and women: Romantic, yet comforting, companion and confidante, and over all your partner for life.

Friends: someone to gossip with, someone to have fun with, someone to share secrets with, and someone to rely on when a situation calls for it.

Business: This type of relationship can be most stressful if it is too complex. Paying attention to what the person says vs. what the person does, can mean two different things. Action may speak louder than words.

Co-workers: Working together to get the job done is the idea thing to do. There are some occasions the co-worker will stab you in the back *(either tell on you or lie on you),* and still smile at you as if everything is alright.

Signs that could come to surface for a relationship of a man and woman are, not being attentive as before, not saying the love words enough as before, regular habits are changed. Coming home late from work most of the time, or going out more often with out you.

Signs that could rise to the surface for friendship are: becoming too interested in a situation, trying to become too involved in the subject, bringing up the topic that really disturbs you all the time.

Signs that a business relationship is not what it seems are: not meeting the deadlines as promised, not living up to his/her part of the bargain. Another good sign is that the person is promising one thing but doing another.

Signs of a co-worker being hellish are: acting strange around you only, saying improper statements around you. Also the co-working is spreading rumors about you that can't be proven; and last but not least lying on you behind your back to others including the boss.

Of course the signs mentioned above, are just some of the signs to look for. There are much more signs that can make themselves more visible. Always remember that signs are there. No matter how large, no matter how small, signs are around. In some cases you may get one small sign, and that is all you get. Pay attention to the signs and let that person know that you are paying attention to them. It may not change anything, but at least you may not be caught off guard. If you see signs in your relationship, it doesn't mean that they are bad. You will have to decide whether the signs are bad or not. Remember, don't read into the situation more than what it is. You can become your worse enemy. Also, in any situation, don't accuse unless you know without a doubt that the signs you see are bad. Don't jump the gun in any situation, because you will become the bad person, and not the person you are accusing.

The one thing that I want to tell certain females is, you really need to know that being long winded doesn't make you right in your prosecutions. It just makes you look like a big mouth idiot. Remember this fact the next time you open you mouth.

Long Winded Females Shut Up!

Have you ever come across a female who just can't shut up in one sentence? Have you ever come across a female who doesn't give you a chance to give an explanation for a certain problem? Females who are long winded are like run on sentences *(like the two above)*. A run on sentence is a long sentence without punctuation. A long winded female is a female who gets as many words in her speech before she can take another breath *(some males are the same way)*. The sentence above starting with *"A long winded female"*, is an example of a run on sentence; and it is a good example of a long winded female.

Long winded females on many occasions, feel they have the upper hand on a person, because of their talent in out talk a person. For the females who have more wind than they do common sense, I have to tell you something. When I tell you this message, please have the courtesy to SHUT THE HELL UP!

Females, who are long winded, miss out on a lot of information that they should learn. This is what they do that is wrong. When speaking to a person (s), they don't give good time response. Let me explain what I mean. You see, long winded females will ask someone a question, and when the other person answers, they cut them off by asking another question. When this is done, the long winded female won't hear the information that she was expecting. The information that she is missing, could have been the information that would have answered her question. This will happen in regular conversations as well as arguments. On many occasions, the long winded female is wrong in her attempts to out talk, or over talk the other person. Then we have the other issue of being loud.

Long winded females have a bad habit of being loud, and over talking the other person. So now we have long winded, loud, and over talking others. It is hard to be civil with a person who is like that. Tempers will fly, and then you have a bigger problem than before.

Long winded females always feel that they are right in every conversation; then they feel they have all the information they need. What they don't realize is, they don't have all of the information, and they could have the wrong information. Then at a later date, they find out what they perceive to be the truth wasn't all the truth, or wasn't the truth at all. So it is important to slow your road. What does that mean? Well to tell you straight out, it means to SHUT THE HELL UP! LISTEN TO WHAT SOMEONE IS TRYING TO TELL YOU! WHEN YOU LISTEN, YOU CAN GET A BETTER PICTURE OF THE SITUATION. YOU WILL ALSO GET A BETTER UNDERSTANDING OF WHAT IS BEING TOLD TO YOU! ALSO, FAST TALKING ADDED TO LONG WINDEDNESS, AND BEING LOUD MAKES YOU A DYSFUNCTIONAL BITCH. I SAY THE WORD BITCH, NOT AS A STREET LANGUAGE, BUT AS DICTIONARY TERM. GET AN UPDATED DICTIONARY, AND LOOK UP THE WORD BITCH. IT DOESN'T JUST MEAN A DOG ANY MORE.

When a female is loud, long winded, added with fast talking, she may find herself with a busted lip in some cases. No one will want to be around this type of female because of her actions. If you find people around this type of female, then two things could be happening. (1) They are loud, long winded, just like her, or (2) they are around her for entertainment purposes only. You may be surprised why people may hang around a dysfunctional person. A female like this may not get any type of sympathy, or support from anyone.

When A Man Takes You For Granted
The Signs Will Be There

Most of the time, a woman's mate will show strong signs that he will or will not do something. These signs are obvious. But let's talk about the signs that are not obvious. These signs are little in size, and can be over looked. Let's get some examples going.

1. You asked your boyfriend if he loved you. He says "Yes, I love you." Then he does something to make you doubt his statement of love. Both of you are together at a restaurant, and he sees a friend. The friend is a female, and he looks at her with special eyes (*that is a sign*).

2. Are we ever going to get married? He thinks for a minute (*a real minute*), and then he doesn't say anything. You are looking for an answer that you can hear. But he doesn't give one. Well ladies, he just gave you an answer. The answer is no. You see, he gave you a non-verbal answer by not saying anything at all. Yes, this is a sign that he doesn't love you enough to marry you. He may not love you at all, because he isn't ready to make that big step. Don't get mad at him. You have no right to try to make someone love (*if you have*

to try to make someone love you, then you've got the wrong mate. Love comes naturally).

3. You love him and he doesn't love you *(this happens a lot)*. Possible signs are: He isn't around you, doesn't call you, he isn't seen with you around certain people. When you do go out together its at night. You don't go out that much. He gives excuses why he can't come over all the time. He comes to see you when he needs money *(this is another big sign)*. Stop putting yourself in this position where you love him and he doesn't love you. Loneliness can make you do a lot of things, but the one thing you have to remember is, it will get worse. When a man doesn't love you, and he just likes you, then that is all it will be. Don't put more into what you see. This is the biggest mistake females do, and that is to take the feelings he has for you, and make it bigger than what it really is. You can't do that ladies. Sometimes when a man sees that you will do anything for him, he begins to use you by taking advantage of you. You in return, let him keep doing it because you have his attention, and that is something you've been trying to get. At this point ladies, you have set yourself up for your down fall that is coming.

The three examples that I have just given you, should help you recognize signs in a better way. Ladies, please do not make the number one mistake females are famous for; that mistake is, to accuse your mate of miss doings and you have no proof. Always have proof when you are going to accuse. Also, you should always remember that men will lie when you have no proof. When I say proof, I mean something that is tangible. Catching him in the act is the best proof you can get.

Now you have to have some common sense here ladies. Some men will lie regardless of your tangible proof. If this ever happens to you, then you have to have common sense enough to either work it out, or just leave him all together. Cut your losses ASAP. Don't be stupid enough to let him keep playing games with you, and you keep letting him back in your life. If you do then you may deserve what he is doing to you. There are many women who let men use them to the end; that is not a good thing at all, and I think that most of you know that. If physical abuse has started, then you must end the relationship immediately. If you ever see signs that abuse *(physical or mental)* is going to happen to you, then you need to make previsions to end the relationship now. The signs are there, you just have to stop letting them pass by you. Pay attention to your relationship. Ladies, you have to understand, having a relationship takes a lot of work on both partners. Most relationships are not equal at all. 50/50 on both sides is a must. I have heard some people say that partners have to give 100% to the relationship. What they don't realize is, you are giving 100% to the relationship if the relationship is carrying 50/50.

Having a relationship means positive team work. Both partners are a team. If you have a team member that isn't doing his/her part, then there is a problem. If the problem isn't taken care of, then it will escalate into something bigger than what the both of you can handle. This is just one of the problems men and women have when trying to have a relationship. It can be hard work if you are not use to giving attention to anyone but yourself.

Always remember, you may be giving up a little bit of freedom when entering into any relationship. You have to ask yourself, do you have the time to give in a relationship, or do you want to give up the freedom you are use to having? These are questions people don't ask themselves before entering into a relationship. These types of questions are very important. These types of questions that you have to ask yourself, will determine if there will be a strong base to start a relationship. Do not run after a man if you are not going to do the work that is needed to maintain a relationship *(you got no business running after a man in the first place)*. Believe it or not ladies, these are signs you disregard every time you want a relationship. When you disregard these signs, you could be setting yourself up for a crumbled relationship.

Don't be doing a lot of things for your man, if you see him hardly doing anything for the relationship *(yes, this is an obvious sign)*. If you stay in the relationship, then you show him a sign. Don't do for him like you use to *(stop letting him use you)*. He will notice the change.

*On This Page Write Down Your Feelings
About Your Relationship.
Then Decide If You Should Keep Him Or
Let Him Go.
Make You Decision!*

For Further Thoughts If You Can't Decide
Write Down What He Does vs. What He Doesn't Do

In This Half Write Down What You Do
vs.
What You Don't Do (Be Honest)

On This Page Write Down Your Thoughts On How
To Make Your Relationship Better.
Remember, No Matter How Good A Relationship Is
You Can Always Improve It.
Write Down Your Goals (Try To Stick To Them).

Understanding The Basics

On the previous four pages, you should have been able to see what condition your relationship is really in. You should have also been able to see if you can make it better. In order to make this project work, you have to be honest with yourself and your answers. Your answers should be honest, and not what you want them to be. Remember, this project is personal, and you have no reason to lie to yourself.

Writing down your feelings about your relationship, what he does vs. what he doesn't do. What you do vs. what you don't do, and last but not least writing down your thoughts on how to make your relationship better. These exercises are designed to make you think about what you are doing. When you understand the basics of the beginning of a relationship, you may be able to make a better decision on picking a relationship. Does that make sense to you? Well, it should make sense, and it really does work. All you have to do is be honest and don't lie to yourself.

Always remember that relationships take hard work, you have to make adjustments in your life, and you have to be willing to give enough time to your partner. Females also have to understand that men need time to themselves, as well as you do; that should be automatic knowledge. Some females tend to be very selfish, and they expect their men to have no time to themselves. Those type of females need to get a grip.

If a female says she can't give him any space because he will drift, then she has the wrong mate. She is trying to force the relationship her way. The relationship is guaranteed to fail, and bad things will happen. This is why it is important to pay attention to the signs that will come up. Signs also are unexpected. Try to recognize them when it happens.

Things To Keep Out Of Your Relationship
Verbal and Physical Abuse

You may have read in the early readings in this publication about abuse, but I want to talk about it again. You see, females have a bad habit of hitting a man, because they want to show they've been hurt by the words or actions of the male. Females want to show the male that they can fight too. Females want to show that they were raised by brothers. There are all kinds of reasons why a female may hit a man.

This is one of the things you seriously need to stop doing. Most females need to stop starting the fights that may happen in a relationship. It is clear that not all females start the fight, but I am speaking about the ones that do. You remember the teachings that men aren't suppose to hit a woman. I agree with that teaching, but that doesn't give the woman the right to put her hands on the male.

I have heard women say that the man should walk away from the female. Well ladies, sometimes it isn't that easy. You know as well as I do, that females can be so bad till heavy escalation happens with the situation. In a situation like that, a male has every right to defend himself.

For the females who have been battered, and verbally abused. I am so sorry that has happened to you, and I wish I can take it away;

but you have to put what has happen to you aside, in order to make the correct decision on another female's situation. So you know what I am talking about, there are many females who have no sympathy for a man when they hear a woman abuse them. The female that has been abused by a male, looks at her own condition, and she can't see pass her own dilemma. Let it be known that I am speaking about survivors of many years. Survivors of one or more years, may not be able to see pass their situation. They need much more time to heal, and in some cases, survivors of 10 years or more are in the same boat. Please remember that some men are in the same situation the females are in with domestic violence. The morale is, you have to *(if you can)* put your own situation aside to see that males go through abuse also.

Think about this for a moment. If you really love each other, then you got no business putting your hands on each other in a harsh way. If the man puts his hands on you in a harsh way *(hit you and you didn't hit him)*, then it is time for you to make plans to leave. The purpose of this talk is to let you know what females did in the old days, isn't the right way to go. Face it ladies, these men now days will knock the hell out of you if you hit them. Keep your hands to yourself, and he should do the same. If real love is present, domestic violence will not be present. Ask yourself this question. Do I really know what love is? If you answered yes to that question, then ask yourself this question. If I know what love is, then why am I dysfunctional, and why is domestic violence present in my life? I know that you may not be honest with your answers, but you need to start taking responsibility for what you do, and stop blaming it on him. All you have to do is to decide if you want to change your character. If you do, then you need to start the process.

(The questions above are for the females who causes trouble in their own relationship, and they can't keep there hands to themselves.)

Summary

In this publication, you have read some very interesting facts about the female race. You the reader have read my going off on certain females, and you the reader, have read applauding facts about certain females. This publication wasn't written to make fun of a female's pride or character. It was written to make females become aware of their reputation. Some reputations are good, some are bad, and then you have the down right pathetic reputations.

It is understood that many females will continue to have bad or pathetic reputations *(it will be hopeless to expect them to change)*. But for the females who want to change, and they are looking for help, then you can say that help has arrived.

I have spoken to specific cultures in this publication, and I meant what I said. Females don't want to talk about the different things that make a female bad. Sometimes females need a wake up call. Of course many will not accept this wake up call, and many will not think that what was said in this publication, reflects on them *(they are mistaken)*. I suggest to all females, that if you think that this publication doesn't reflect you in some way, then you need to think again.

Remember, this is a guide to improve a woman's self respect. It is personal, private and serious; and it should be taken as such. Valuable information is in this publication, and I pray this publication can help the females in need. For others, I tried.

Respect each other no matter what race you are in, and respect others no matter what. Ladies, we all need to join together and reclaim our self respect, and society will see the change. Let's go for it!

A Meeting With The Both Of You

I just want to get the females and the males together so they can see that both sides have faults that need to be corrected. Both sides always talk about each other. The sad part is that neither one of you can throw a stone. Both sides have to do some major cleaning in their house. I can try to lead you to the truth, but it will be up to the both of you to make a stand, and claim what is yours.

If you want to read more, feel free to order "Relationships"

"Relationships"
It's Time For A Change
48 page pamphlet book
$6.50

Name:_____

Address: _____

City: _____ St:_____ Zip:_____

Send Ck or Mo to
MG Resources 2305 Park Ave. Ste.
1208 Detroit, Mi. 48201
Phone: (Area Code) _____-_____-_____
(Optional)

Please Allow 2 Weeks for Delivery

About the Author

Madena Williams who is the author of A New Beginning, resides with her husband in Detroit, Michigan. At the age of 45, Mrs. Williams has two adult children (ages 20 and 21), and a three year old granddaughter. She holds a BBA in Management from Davenport University. Other publishings (pamphlet book) are "Relationships" It's Time For A Change, and Relationship surveys.

Mrs. Williams is also a 25 yr survivor of domestic violence (present husband NOT included).